What is a Biblical Worldview?

Foundational Truths

© Copyright 2023 – Andrew Wommack Ministries

Printed in the United States of America. All rights reserved. No portion of this book may be reproduced, stored in a retrieval system, or transmitted in any form or by any means—electronic, mechanical, photocopy, recording, scanning, or other—except for brief quotations in critical reviews or articles, without the prior written permission of the publisher.

Unless otherwise indicated, all Scripture quotations are taken from the King James Version® of the Bible. Copyright © by the British Crown. Public domain.

All emphasis within Scripture quotations is the author's own.

Published in partnership between Andrew Wommack Ministries and Harrison House Publishers.

Woodland Park, CO 80863 – Shippensburg, PA 17257

ISBN 13 TP: 978-1-59548-617-2

For Worldwide Distribution, Printed in the USA

1 2 3 4 5 6 / 26 25 24 23

CONTENTS

Introduction 1

Chapter 1 How Important Is a Biblical Worldview? ... 7

Chapter 2 The Bible Is the Inspired, Accurate Word of God 13

Chapter 3 Biblical Creationism 19

Chapter 4 The True Nature of God 27

Chapter 5 The Fallen Nature of Man 33

Chapter 6 You New Identity in Christ 39

Conclusion 45

Receive Jesus as Your Savior 49

Receive the Holy Spirit 51

Note: This booklet is just a brief introduction to Andrew's twelve hours of teaching from *the Biblical Worldview: Foundational Truths* curriculum. Statistics included in the "Did You Know?" sections of this booklet were cited when the complete curriculum was originally published and may no longer represent the most current information.

INTRODUCTION

Everyone views the world based on their beliefs—it's their worldview. As you process everything that you encounter, whether you know it or not, you are looking at it through a lens based on a variety of influences. You filter life based on experiences and factors from your background, such as where you grew up, family dynamics, ethnic heritage, religious upbringing, education and educators' views shared with students, and political views. Every day, your worldview guides your thoughts, decisions, and conversations.

It may surprise you to know that Christians don't automatically have a biblical worldview. When you became a Christian, you just began a journey to renew your mind. You did not automatically get a biblical worldview download at salvation. The problem many Christians face is a clash of worldviews. Often, it is difficult to recognize the daily assault on their Christian values and biblical teachings. Take note the next time you hear a news report or people sharing their perspectives and if you feel a twinge inside that indicates something isn't sitting right in your spirit. Typically, people are busy and ignore that twinge. When someone regularly encounters and hears perspectives that conflict with God's truth, that person can become dulled to it and simply begin to accept those perspectives as truth.

Other times, the assault on biblical truth is blatant and very clear that what is being presented isn't something a Christian can endorse or internalize. For example, any true Christian knows that the LGBTQ+ propaganda that is being shoved down our throats is wrong. It is not consistent with what the Bible says. But what should Christians do or say? Aren't Christians supposed to be meek and mild and get along with everybody?

Jesus Christ didn't encourage His followers to hide within the church's four walls. We are to go into all the world and make disciples (Matt. 28:19-20). As followers of Christ, our mission entails sharing the truth about Jesus and salvation, but first we need to know the truth. Jesus said, *"I am the way, the truth, and the life"* (John 14:6). We come to know that truth from the Bible.

Sharing the Gospel is vital, but we can't ignore sinful and unrighteous leaders who create environments hostile to it, seeking to destroy families, especially children. Jesus loves children (Matt. 19:14), but Satan has orchestrated major attacks on children to keep them from hearing and accepting Christ as Savior. When Christians know and live their biblical worldview, they can become a beacon of light to share the love and truth of Christ to a hurting world.

So, how do you build a biblical worldview? A biblical worldview comes from knowing God's word on any issue or topic pertaining to life. Just as you strive for your actions to reflect Christ's influence and resemble Him, your worldview should depend on using God's Word as a filter, so you'll act and think differently than those who are influenced by a non-biblical worldview.

This booklet gives you an overview of six key areas that are foundational to build a biblical worldview. Your biblical foundation is built through hearing and reading God's Word and applying it to your life. This booklet will also introduce you to how legalistic Christianity and secular culture have distorted the truth about God and man. You will be guided to look at scriptures and see how to think, act, and speak God's truth about issues in today's world. Now, more than ever, people need to hear the truth that will set them free—and you can influence them as you learn and live with a biblical worldview!

CHAPTER 1
HOW IMPORTANT IS A BIBLICAL WORLDVIEW?

Your worldview is a way of looking at things—a paradigm. It's also a way of thinking and processing that shapes everything you experience in life. As a Christian, a biblical worldview is very important, and it will influence the way you see things compared to people who aren't Christians and who don't have a biblical worldview.

Consider the contrasting worldviews of two Germans who both died in April 1945, Dietrich Bonhoeffer and Adolf Hitler. Bonhoeffer, a German clergyman, could have safely stayed in the U.S. during World War II, but he realized that he owed it to his fellow citizens to go back to Germany and resist Hitler. When he returned, Hitler imprisoned him and sentenced him to death.[1] His biblical worldview allowed him to preach while imprisoned and view death as "the beginning of life."[1] A mere twenty-one days after Bonhoeffer's execution, a greatly distressed Hitler who had been in hiding, committed suicide in his underground bunkers.[2]

Both of these men lived at the same time, in the same country, and both faced death just days apart. Bonhoeffer faced death with courage, while Hitler went out with a whimper. Their worldviews made the difference.

We must be on guard; we are in a war of worldviews. A lot of people don't understand this, but there is evil in our world. Satan is real, and whether you know it or not, we are at war (Eph. 6:12–13). There is a real battle going on, and Satan intends to come and spoil us. The word *spoil* isn't talking about the way that meat or fruit spoils. It is talking about when you go out, fight an enemy at war, kill your enemy, and then you take their treasures. We have riches in Christ (Eph. 3:8), and we need to guard against their loss.

In today's technological age, I believe Christians are being fought against more than any group of Christians that have ever existed on this planet. We are being bombarded. Our news media is not just reporting what is happening, but it's the "evening prophecy" striking fear in people's hearts about what's coming. If you don't have a biblical worldview or know what God says about how this earth is going to end, then you'll buy into the scare tactics. Jesus gave us His Word to counteract the fear and lies. People are worrying and forecasting tragedies and things that do not line up with what the Bible says is going to happen (Luke 21:26).

If you have a biblical worldview, instead of being terrified or afraid when you see signs of the times coming to pass, you can look at them and take comfort that the return of the Lord is coming. You can have a totally different response (Acts 1:10–11; 1 John 2:28; Rev. 22:12, 20).

> **DID YOU KNOW?**
> In 2019, only about 52% of millennials identified as Christian.[3] In 2020, a poll showed only 64% of Americans identified as Christian, down from 90% in 1970.[4]

Statistics show the need for a biblical worldview. In 1892, the United States Supreme Court said that America is a Christian nation.[5] Even fifty years ago, the influence of the church was so great that people who didn't know, love, or live for God still had knowledge of Him. That influence has completely eroded today. Most people are being influenced more by our secular culture than they are by the Bible.

Sadly, the church has failed to teach biblical morality as commanded in 1 Peter 3:15,

But sanctify the Lord God in your hearts: and be ready always to give an answer to every man that asketh you a reason of the hope that is in you with meekness and fear."

The word *answer* comes from the Greek word *apologia*, and it's where we get the word *apologetics*.[6] When you're talking about Christian apologetics, you aren't talking about apologizing for something but rather being able to give a defense or an answer for what the Bible has to say. The body of Christ must get outside of the four walls of our church buildings, and we've got to get into education and into society. People did not like what the apostle Paul said, but he kept saying it. If you truly love a person, then you are going to be able to confront them with the truth.

It's the truth that sets people free (John 8:32), but it's only the truth that they *know* that makes them free. I do not have the right to reject the truth for them. I've got to tell them the truth—and do so in love because the Bible teaches love, not tolerance (John 2:15; Gal. 1:8-9).

God's Word will give you direction and show you what you need to do. Many people are stumbling today because they don't have the light of God's Word. Our whole lives must be dominated and controlled by what the Word of God says, and very few Christians let the Bible get in the way of what they believe. If we don't shine the light and preserve the influence of the Gospel, then there is no other hope. The only hope that we have is to return to the Word of God.

The Bible has instructions about your personal life, your relationship with the Lord and with others, and every aspect of life. There is something in the Word of God to answer any issue that you're dealing with. And once you know what the Word says, you can begin forming a biblical worldview.

CHAPTER 2
THE BIBLE IS THE INSPIRED, ACCURATE WORD OF GOD

To have a biblical worldview, you must believe that the entire Bible is inspired and 100 percent accurate. The Bible is not a book that men wrote about God. The Bible is what God inspired men to write about Him. The authority of God's Word is clearly explained in 2 Timothy 3:16–17,

All scripture is *given by inspiration of God, and* is *profitable for doctrine, for reproof, for correction, for instruction in righteousness: That the man of God may be perfect, throughly furnished unto all good works.*

You can't subscribe to some of it and ignore inconvenient or politically incorrect parts. Some people say, "I believe in the Bible," but they reject what the Bible has to say about creation. They reject the idea that we were created on purpose and designed by a creator; and they just accept evolution. That is not a biblical worldview.

The Bible is unique among all books. First of all, the Bible was written over a span of 1,500 years by forty different people from multiple nations and written in multiple languages.[7] There are 66,000 biblical manuscripts compared with only 1,900 copies of Homer's *Iliad*[8] (the second most copied ancient manuscript). There are only a handful of documents that talk about Julius Caesar and some coins with his inscription on them. We have more documentation of the life, ministry, death, and resurrection of the Lord Jesus Christ than we have proving that Julius Caesar even lived.[9]

If you compared the number of manuscripts, the detail, and the confirmation we have of the Word of God to the documents we have about other facts in history that are undisputed, you'd see that the Bible is infinitely more accurate. The reason this is important is because in the fifty years following the events of Jesus' life, death, and resurrection, there were still people alive who witnessed these things. If there had been errors in the New Testament manuscripts, then some of the eyewitnesses would have spoken up, and yet that didn't happen. Just the opposite, those scriptures were quoted so often among the early Church that the silence of any critics coming against them is a tremendous testimony to their accuracy. The four Gospels were referenced so many times that all but eleven verses could be reassembled without the originals.

The Bible contains over 300 prophecies about the coming of Jesus that were prophesied hundreds of years before—yet came to pass perfectly.[10] It's extremely improbable that one person could fulfill even 100 prophecies, but Jesus fulfilled 300. To anyone who has an open mind and will honestly consider all these claims, this is infallible proof in the accuracy of the Bible.[10]

Of all the unique prophecies about Jesus' birth, Isaiah 7:14 dared prophesy that *"a virgin shall conceive, and bear a son, and shall call his name Immanuel."* Confirmation of this prophecy is found in both Matthew 1:23 and Luke 1:26-27, 31. It's amazing that the Bible would prophesy that the Son of God would come in some kind of body that wasn't perfect. Outwardly, Jesus was normal, not beautiful or a dominant person. Psalm 22:7-8 prophesied that God Himself would be despised, rejected, and people would mock Him. The fulfillment is verified in Matthew 27:43 and Luke 23:35. The fact that the birth and life of Jesus came to pass exactly as prophesied is strong confirmation that the Bible is not men writing about God but God writing through men.

Because of these truths, and so many others, any person who doesn't take the Bible into consideration and use it to form a worldview is

> **DID YOU KNOW?**
>
> Art, music, freedom, justice, equal rights, work ethic, virtues of self-reliance, and self-discipline came from the influence of the Bible and Christianity upon the world. The Bible also influenced Galileo, Sir Isaac Newton, and Christopher Columbus, as well as America's first universities: Harvard, Princeton, and Yale.

intellectually dishonest. The Bible talks about people who are willingly ignorant. There are a lot of people who do not examine the claims of the Bible, and the reason is because they don't want the truth, the morality, and the light of the Bible affecting their actions (2 Pet. 3:5). People choose to be ignorant about the Bible because they don't want it to get in the way of what they're doing. The kingdom of God is dependent upon the Bible. To have a biblical worldview, you must believe that the Word of God is divinely inspired and accurate in all its ways.

CHAPTER 3
BIBLICAL CREATIONISM

The Bible and evolution are incompatible. Evolution is the weapon that strikes at our belief that we were created and designed; that we have purpose and accountability, not only to God but to other people.

Sadly, people love their immorality. They know the Word of God stands against this, so they willingly embrace evolution as a justification that everything is relative. They believe there isn't a God who has a perfect standard, and each one of us is free to come up with what is right for ourselves. That's relativism, or what the Bible would call idolatry. Instead of acknowledging God's standards, they make themselves a god and choose for themselves what is right and wrong.

Evolution is a theory, not an established fact. It is absolutely dependent upon random things happening; however, many scientists are saying that the universe leads us to the conclusion that life was not random. It *was* planned, it *was* designed, and it *is* supernatural. It takes more faith to believe in evolution than it does to believe in a God who created everything. People who believe in evolution have a predisposition against God, and I believe it is demonically motivated. Satan is behind it, whether they know it or not. He is the one who has given them the desire to disbelieve the witness of creation.

Although schools teach that man evolved from an ape, there has never been a link found that shows man developing from apes.[11] Once you reduce yourself to an animal with no accountability to a creator, then all fear is removed. Psalm 36:1 affirms a link between a lack of fear of God and wickedness:

The transgression of the wicked saith within my heart, that there is no fear of God before his eyes.

In Genesis 1, it says four different times that God gave the animals and the sea creatures the ability to produce after their kind. You can't make a dog out of a whale. You can't change species. There is no evidence of this occurring, and there never will be.

> **DID YOU KNOW?**
>
> Over the past 150 years, evolutionist Charles Darwin's The Origin of Species has influenced Planned Parenthood founder Margaret Sanger, along with communist dictators like China's Mao Zedong, Cambodia's Pol Pot, and the former Soviet Union's Joseph Stalin. It is estimated that more than 60 million unborn children have been killed by abortion in the United States since 1973, and communism has caused more than 100 million deaths worldwide since 1900.

Scientists say the earth is millions of years old, but there are many examples in nature to the contrary. For example, Mount St. Helens erupted in 1980, and seventy-five feet of deposits were laid down in just a matter of hours.[12] These deposits match the different strata of the earth which evolutionists say took millions of years to form. Evolutionists said that after Mount St. Helens, the destroyed vegetation would take tens of thousands of years to be restored. I've seen a report that after twenty years, it had already recovered.[13]

Some believe in theistic evolution—that God controlled evolution and that it happened over millions and millions of years.[14] But if you stretched theistic evolution to say that for millions of years things had been progressing up until man, that is contrary to Scripture that says death came into the world through Adam. There couldn't have been this cycle of death and rebirth along with mutations and improvement in the gene pool over the millions of years. A theistic evolution mindset, or any type of evolution mindset, leads to believing that you aren't created in the image of God; you're just a man that's evolved. Therefore, we don't have any accountability to a creator, and we don't need to follow some arbitrary standard that the Bible puts down. Each of us can establish what's right and wrong.

Dr. Carl Baugh was a theistic evolutionist. He was a Christian, but he believed that God controlled evolution over long periods of time. He was a professor and led one of his classes to do an excavation on the Paluxy River in Glen Rose, Texas. They uncovered dinosaur prints that had a human footprint inside of the dinosaur print. They were imposed on the same piece of clay that was excavated, and this is what turned him towards believing that there was a literal creation; and now he has the Creation Evidence

Museum.[15] Watch Andrew's interview with Dr. Baugh: **awmi.net/Dr.Baugh** (Week 17 - Episodes 3 & 4; Week 18 - Episodes 6 & 9; and Week 19 - Episode 11).

If you are going to truly be scientific and let the facts dictate, then you can't exclude any possibilities. You can't exclude the possibility that God created man on purpose and designed us. There are thousands of scientists who say creation and nature led them to the conclusion that there must be a creator,[16] but you don't have to be a rocket scientist to come to this same conclusion. A creator can be found in creation stories from civilizations around the world; people have seen the witness of creation (Ps. 19:1–4). Since the most basic definition of life is the ability to reproduce, and since all our earthly resources can't create life, then a person is an absolute fool to think life happened accidentally.

We were created by God, and Genesis 1:27 shows that we were created in God's image:

So God created man in his own image, in the image of God created he him; male and female created he them.

We are His image bearers and are going to answer to God. The Word of God is true, and we've got to believe in biblical creationism. Every person knows there must be something bigger than themselves that created them.

When people get away from a fear of God and an understanding of who He is, what His standards are, and what He is holding us accountable for, they choose to live in sin. This is happening in epidemic proportions today because the Word of God has been taken away—a lack of a biblical worldview or standard of morality is enabling these things. We need to take the Bible literally. We need to believe it, and we need to reject evolution (Matt. 12:33). We cannot compromise on this issue, or it's going to take us down a road that we will regret.

CHAPTER 4
THE TRUE NATURE OF GOD

A biblical worldview is based on believing God's Word, and it is through God's Word that we come to know Him. You cannot have a relationship with a person if you don't understand what their nature and character are like. If you know the true nature of God, you won't be fooled and believe anything that differs from His nature. You will also recognize when a worldview distorts it.

Religion has misrepresented God by teaching that God is absolutely sovereign and nothing happens without God controlling or willing it. God does not control everything. I believe in sovereignty the way the dictionary defines it, meaning first in rank, order, or authority; supreme in authority. I believe that God is absolutely the top of the food chain, and nobody can force Him to do anything. He does whatever He wants to. God is absolute, but He gave people free will. He willed the children of Israel to go into the Promised Land (Ps. 78:41). But they disbelieved God, and God judged them; so they spent forty years in the wilderness (Josh. 5:6). God didn't ordain that. They chose that through their disobedience.

A person who believes that God ultimately controls everything will teach you to submit to everything because it's God's will. However, some things are of the devil, and the Bible tells us to resist them (James 4:7). If you believe that God controls everything, there would be no such thing as resisting the devil and having him flee from us.

There are religious people who have been taught the Word, but they've been taught a wrong representation of the Word that does not accurately represent Him. That's not good.

People disappointed with something that's going on in their life or in culture believe that God is bad because of it—they feel justified in rejecting Him. That is not the proper way to approach God. People who understand the true nature of God and know that He is a good God go through tragedy without blaming Him. They just say, "Father, teach me what I don't know. Help me to understand." They take what the Word of God reveals about His true nature, and they don't become offended.

Another aspect of God's true nature is that He is love. It's not one of His attributes; it's His core. In 1 John 4:8, we find this foundational truth:

He that loveth not knoweth not God; for God is love.

He isn't harsh and angry like people characterize God based on the Old Testament. Early in the Old Testament, people had mistaken

God's lack of punishment and lack of rejection for sin as approval. This caused sin to escalate. God gave the law to drive people to the end of themselves so they would cry out to Him for salvation. God loved us and wanted to deal in mercy with us, but He couldn't do it without paying for our sins. Jesus became a man, and Jesus drew all of God's judgment (God's wrath) onto Him when He was lifted up on the cross (John 12:32). Jesus took that judgment so that now under the New Covenant, we have a relationship with God that people under the Old Covenant could only dream of.

People look at the harsh way God punished sin in the Old Testament Law and think that was the true nature of God. No, the true nature of God is that He didn't impute man's sins unto them.

God wasn't holding people's sins against them until the Law came. He was being merciful (Rom. 5:13). There was mercy and grace on people under the Old Testament before the Law was given. Noah was righteous because he put faith in God, and God gave him righteousness (Gen. 6:8-9). Abraham believed God, and it was counted unto him for righteousness (Gen. 15:6). These men weren't perfect, yet God dealt with them in mercy. You don't see this after the Law was given. There is a huge distinction between the way God dealt with sin in the Old Testament and the way He deals with it in the New Testament—and the difference is not because God has changed. The way that He deals with us has changed because of what Jesus did.

When you misunderstand God's true nature and character, you try to relate to God based on your performance. God is love, and God wants to deal with us in love, but He's also holy and just. Until you accept the payment that Jesus made for your sins, you'll have to relate to God based on your own goodness. But the moment you make Jesus your Lord and become born again, you become a new creature and have a relationship with God (2 Cor. 5:17). You need to understand that Jesus paid for your sins, and God is no longer angry with you. He isn't even condemning you. He loves you so much and doesn't want you to live under guilt, shame, and condemnation.

When you filter life through the biblical worldview lens that knows God's true nature, you will recognize that God loves people and isn't sending evil or causing harm. You will speak truth to people who insist that God controls everything. You will choose to become involved in bringing God's truth to situations in the church where some simply believe that it must be God's will for the bad things that are happening in the world. But what a blessing that God reveals His true nature so we can know He will never stop loving us!

CHAPTER 5
THE FALLEN NATURE OF MAN

The devil has misrepresented God's true nature, which has led people to have a wrong opinion about themselves and about God. If you don't fully appreciate what Jesus saved you from, then you will not have a full appreciation of what you have in Christ. Deception about man's true fallen nature becomes distorted through a godless worldview. By understanding the fallen nature of man, a person's worldview shifts to the understanding that they are not good enough for heaven and need a savior.

Often people just turn to the Lord when they are in trouble. When it comes to physical things, people tend to take their health for granted and don't think about it until they get sick—then they seek the Lord. The time to build your house upon the rock (Matt. 7:24-27) is not when the storm is raging and you're in a battle for your life. You need to build your house while the sun is shining and everything is good. You don't have to let Satan literally destroy your life before you realize that you are headed in the wrong direction. You need to be looking unto Jesus, the author and the finisher of your faith, and find out who you are in Him. When you look back at the mess you were in before you met the Lord, remember to praise God because you have been forgiven of so much.

Early in my life, I had a revelation of God's true nature and my sinful, fallen nature—it changed my life. I had lived a relatively holy life, and developed a "Pharisee syndrome," where I thought I was better than other people. I felt like I deserved God's goodness in my life, and it was all about me. I was leading people to the Lord so I could receive praise from people. I wasn't doing it for God.

In a prayer meeting on March 23, 1968, all of a sudden, it was like God drew back a curtain. He opened up my eyes and showed me what an absolute hypocrite I was. All the witnessing I was doing, my holy living, my prayer—everything was for the praise of other people.

God showed me that I was a modern-day Pharisee. I was taught that if you did wrong and sinned, then God was liable to put sickness on you. He was liable to kill somebody close to you. When I saw myself as a religious hypocrite and saw the self-righteousness I had in me, I honestly thought God was going to kill me. I saw myself in relation to His perfect standard, and I saw myself as an absolute sinner. Then, the glory of God came into that place as God revealed Himself to me. The glory of God and His perfect standard revealed that all my righteousness was like a filthy rag (Isa. 64:6). When I saw my fallen nature, I began to confess everything in the hopes that if God killed me, I'd go to heaven instead of hell.

My theology was very immature at that time, and I know that's wrong on a number of levels. But I'm just telling you this is what I thought. I began to turn myself inside out. Instead of having God's wrath come upon me, I had a supernatural, tangible love of God come and fill me. It transformed my life because I began to see an accurate picture of who I was in Christ and the power and the authority that I have through Him.

Many people view humanity as basically good and don't understand the fallen nature of man. But God's Word clearly shows that people at their core are evil because they are born with a sin nature. A child left to his own will bring his mother to shame (Prov. 29:15). If you leave that child to his own, I guarantee you, they will grow up to be a "hell raiser." It will destroy them.

Since people are evil (Jer. 17:9; Eph. 2:2–3) and in need of a savior, everyone must understand the fallen nature of mankind, or it will lead to

> **Did You Know?**
> Christianity is the only religion that has a savior. Every other religion requires you to save yourself by conforming your actions and thoughts.

self-salvation. They will think that they are good enough, that God is going to accept them based on their performance, and that they have a free ticket into heaven. But only people who recognize their need for forgiveness and receive salvation through Jesus go to heaven. You can't rely on yourself to be good and do good, but you need to recognize that in Christ, you can do all things (Phil. 4:13). You also need to recognize that without Christ, you can do nothing (John 15:5). You need to have both of those things in balance. If you can understand that your spirit is perfect and your flesh isn't, then when you do make a mistake, it won't totally devastate you. Your flesh (mind, will, and emotions) isn't saved, so don't rely on it; but live out of who you are in Christ, and let Him live through you.

You see, the answer to the world's problems is not to eradicate poverty or prejudice. These problems are caused by what's in people's hearts. We are by nature a child of the devil until we are born again. That's why the Lord established government to be a terror to those who do evil works and to cause them to withdraw from their sin (Rom. 13:1-4). Law and government are a restraint on sin because man's nature leads him to sin. In a society without God, people don't have any internal restraints. You can't put enough laws on the outside to control them. You need to have your heart changed and recognize that you need a savior. We see our society going in a bad direction because people are getting away from the Word of God and God's standards. Ultimately, they're getting away from a biblical worldview—a biblical standard of morality.

CHAPTER 6
YOUR NEW IDENTITY IN CHRIST

When you don't understand what the Bible says about salvation leading to a new identity in Christ, you might operate from a worldview that doesn't know you are an overcomer in your spirit. For example, I knew that I was born again, yet in the flesh, old things hadn't passed away and all things hadn't become new (2 Cor. 5:17). There were so many things that I wanted to change in my life, and I wasn't seeing those changes. As I tried to understand this, the Lord led me to 1 Thessalonians 5:23,

> *... and I* pray God *your whole spirit and soul and body be preserved blameless unto the coming of our Lord Jesus Christ.*

> **Did You Know?**
>
> Most people think that *spirit* and *soul* are interchangeable, but that's not so according to 1 Thessalonians 5:23.

This is one of the clearest verses that states you have a spirit, soul, and body.

I realized that there was a third part to me: my spirit, even though I can't see it. And God's Word is a perfect representation of what our spirit is like (John 6:63). But it's the physical and the emotional part of us that we are constantly in touch with. Despite this, you can't go by just your feelings, your emotions, and what you see. You can't go by what you taste, hear, smell, or feel either.

People mistakably think that if we have the power of God living on the inside, then we will automatically know it. No, we won't. You need to trust the Word of God as much as what you can sense through your eyes, hear through your ears, and feel through your body. You must use a sixth sense—faith—to determine what's happening on the inside of you.

Your body and your soul are not changed yet—you aren't a new physical creature. But in your spirit, you are a brand-new person; the old nature is gone. But left behind is a body of wrong thinking, wrong feelings, wrong attitudes, and a wrong worldview. That's why you have to look to the Word of God to see who you really are in the spirit and change the way that you think.

No one can claim that their physical body and their mental and emotional part are as Jesus is right now. However, in your spirit, you are one with the Lord (1 Cor. 6:17). The Greek word for *one* is *heis*.[18] You are not just parallel or similar. It's not like God's up there and your spirit is down here. No, you are one. They are identical.

The moment you believed in Christ, you were sealed with the Holy Spirit (Eph. 1:13). When you sin as a Christian, that sin enters into your physical body. It can give Satan an inroad to your life, and anything that's in the physical realm is open to attack. Sin can also make you spiritually blind, cause you not to think straight, and even harden your heart toward God. But even though you sin, that sin doesn't affect your spirit.

Before salvation, sin and emotions ruled your life. A transformation needs to take place to reflect your new identity in Christ. Those wrong feelings can sometimes make you think God doesn't love you. When you don't feel His love, don't say, "Oh God, would you please just pour out your love in my life? Would you show me that you love me?" This thinking assumes that if you don't feel God's love, then it must not exist. Actually, that is unbelief; it's an indication of how carnal you are. Most people think that being carnal means being a terrible sinner—vile and ungodly. But the word *carnal* just means dominated by the five senses.

If you are going to believe God, then you have to believe that He never changes in His love toward you because He's looking at you in the spirit. Your spirit is sealed by the Holy Spirit—there are no impurities—and He loves you as if you've never sinned. God fellowships with you based on what Jesus did and based upon your faith in Him. He loves you and doesn't want you to open up a door to the devil.

You may be thinking, *What does this have to do with worldview?* Well, your sin nature was dominant in you up until the time you became born again, and it programmed and taught you your worldview. Now that you are born again, you have to reprogram your thinking with these truths of God's Word. Since the real you is a spirit being, you need to start living out of your spirit. Renewing your mind will lead to a biblical way of looking at things, ultimately forming the foundation of your biblical worldview.

CONCLUSION

As sin becomes more rampant in today's culture, and deviant behaviors signal society's moral decline, it becomes more important to discern truth and identify what contradicts your biblical worldview. When you completely trust God's Word, you are armed with a valuable compass for your life. Knowing the foundational truths of who God is and who you are in Christ equips you to stand firm on the truths from God's Word.

What happens when you recognize an opposing worldview? Will you stand up for truth and boldly proclaim what God's Word says? Don't remain silent because you don't know everything the Word says. The Holy Spirit will guide you and reveal truth.

No longer can the church sit by silently and watch today's culture be guided by a godless, secular worldview. Pray for the Holy Spirit to lead you to opportunities to stand up for truth and get involved in bringing God's truth to light in our world.

CONTINUE BUILDING YOUR BIBLICAL WORLDVIEW

Every day, you are confronted with non-biblical worldviews coming to you through social media, the internet, and secular news sources. The **Truth and Liberty Coalition (www.truthandliberty.net)** can guide you to process current events through the lens of God's Word.

- *Live Call-in Show:* insight on current issues and callers can ask questions about biblical worldview or any topic
- *Website:* resources include a 24/7 news feed, links to other online content related to biblical worldview and current American government issues, blogs, voter guides, and prayer guides

If you enjoyed this booklet and would like more tools to arm yourself with a biblical worldview, I suggest these teachings:

- *Biblical Worldview: Foundational Truths* (complete curriculum)
- *What Is Truth?*
- *The True Nature of God*
- *Biblical Worldview* series

Some of these teachings are available for free at **awmi.net**, or they can be purchased at **awmi.net/store**.

RECEIVE JESUS AS YOUR SAVIOR

Choosing to receive Jesus Christ as your Lord and Savior is the most important decision you'll ever make!

God's Word promises, *"That if thou shalt confess with thy mouth the Lord Jesus, and shalt believe in thine heart that God hath raised him from the dead, thou shalt be saved. For with the heart man believeth unto righteousness; and with the mouth confession is made unto salvation"* (Rom. 10:9-10). *"For whosoever shall call upon the name of the Lord shall be saved"* (Rom. 10:13). By His grace, God has already done everything to provide salvation. Your part is simply to believe and receive.

Pray out loud: "Jesus, I confess that You are my Lord and Savior. I believe in my heart that God raised You from the dead. By faith in Your Word, I receive salvation now. Thank You for saving me."

The very moment you commit your life to Jesus Christ, the truth of His Word instantly comes to pass in your spirit. Now that you're born again, there's a brand-new you!

Please contact us and let us know that you've prayed to receive Jesus as your Savior. We'd like to send you some free materials to help you on your new journey. Call our Helpline: **719-635-1111** (available 24 hours a day, seven days a week) to speak to a staff member who is here to help you understand and grow in your new relationship with the Lord.

Welcome to your new life!

RECEIVE THE HOLY SPIRIT

As His child, your loving heavenly Father wants to give you the supernatural power you need to live a new life. *"For every one that asketh receiveth; and he that seeketh findeth; and to him that knocketh it shall be opened...how much more shall your heavenly Father give the Holy Spirit to them that ask him?"* (Luke 11:10-13).

All you have to do is ask, believe, and receive!

Pray this: "Father, I recognize my need for Your power to live a new life. Please fill me with Your Holy Spirit. By faith, I receive it right now. Thank You for baptizing me. Holy Spirit, You are welcome in my life."

Some syllables from a language you don't recognize will rise up from your heart to your mouth (1 Cor. 14:14). As you speak them out loud by faith, you're releasing God's power from within and building yourself up in the spirit (1 Cor. 14:4). You can do this whenever and wherever you like.

It doesn't really matter whether you felt anything or not when you prayed to receive the Lord and His Spirit. If you believed in your heart that you received, then God's Word promises you did. *"Therefore I say unto you, What things soever ye desire, when ye pray, believe that ye receive* **them**, *and ye shall have* **them**" (Mark 11:24). God always honors His Word—believe it!

We would like to rejoice with you and help you understand more fully what has taken place in your life!

Please contact us to let us know that you've prayed to be filled with the Holy Spirit and to request the book *The New You & the Holy Spirit*. This book will explain in more detail about the benefits of being filled with the Holy Spirit and speaking in tongues. Call our Helpline: **719-635-1111** (available 24 hours a day, seven days a week).

CALL FOR PRAYER

If you need prayer for any reason, you can call our Helpline, 24 hours a day, seven days a week at **719-635-1111**. A trained prayer minister will answer your call and pray with you.

Every day, we receive testimonies of healings and other miracles from our Helpline, and we are ministering God's nearly-too-good-to-be-true message of the Gospel to more people than ever. So, I encourage you to call today!

ENDNOTES

1. Stephen J. Nichols, "This Day in History: The Execution of Dietrich Bonhoeffer," *Crossway*, April 9, 2018, https://www.crossway.org/ articles/this-day-in-history-the-execution-of-dietrich-bonhoeffer/.

2. "Adolf Hitler Commits Suicide in His Underground Bunker," *A&E Television Networks*, last updated April 26, 2019, accessed June 2, 2023, https://www.history.com/this-day-in-history/adolf-hitler-commits-suicide.

3. Joe Carter, "To Change America, Invite a Millennial to Church," *The Gospel Coalition*, October 26, 2019, https://www.thegospelcoalition.org/article/to-change-america-invite-a-millenial-to-church/.

4. "Modeling the Future of Religion in America," Pew Research Center, September 13, 2022, https://www.pewresearch.org/religion/2022/09/13/modeling-the-future-of-religion-in-america/.

5. William Federer, "Supreme Court — America a Christian Nation," *The Patriot Post*, April 1, 2019, https://patriotpost.us/opinion/62099-supreme-court-america-a-christian-nation-2019-04-01.

6. *Thayer's Greek Lexicon*, s.v. "ἀπολογία" ("ap-ol-og-ee'-ah"), accessed June 2, 2023, https://www.blueletterbible.org/lexicon/g627/kjv/tr/0-1/.

7. Donna Jones, "The Bible: What Is It, Who Wrote It, and Why It Still Matters Today," Crosswalk.com, July 09, 2019, https://www.biblestudytools.com/bible-study/explore-the-bible/the-bible-what-is-it-who-wrote-it-and-why-it-still-matters-today.html.

8. Josh McDowell and Sean McDowell PhD, *Evidence that Demands a Verdict*, (Nashville: Thomas Nelson, 2017), 57.

9. Darrell Bock, "Sources for Caesar and Jesus Compared," *The Gospel Coalition*, June 11, 2015, https://www.thegospelcoalition.org/article/sources-for-caesar-and-jesus-compared/.

10. "Did Jesus Fulfill Old Testament Prophecy?," *Josh McDowell Ministry*, accessed June 2, 2023, https://www.josh.org/jesus-fulfill-prophecy/.

11. Roger Patterson, "The Importance of Missing Links," Answers in Genesis, accessed June 2, 2023, https://answersingenesis.org/human-evolution/ape-man/importance-missing-links/.

12. "1980 Cataclysmic Eruption," *United States Geological Survey*, https://www.usgs.gov/volcanoes/mount-st.-helens/1980-cataclysmic-eruption.

13. "Life Returns Quickly to Areas Devastated by Mount St. Helens," *New York Times*, March 14,1984, https://www.nytimes.com/1984/03/14/us/life-returns-quickly-to-areas-devastated-by-mount-st-helens.html.

14. Dr. Terry Mortenson, "Theistic Evolution Is Not the Real Problem!," Answers in Genesis, February 1, 2023, https://answersingenesis.org/theistic-evolution/theistic-evolution-not-the-real-problem/.

15. Carl Baugh, *Footprints in Stone*, https://www.footprintsinstone.com.

16. Sharon Begley, "Science Finds God," Newsweek, July 20, 1998, https://www.washingtonpost.com/wp-srv/newsweek/science_of_god/scienceofgod.htm.

17. *Blue Letter Bible*, s.v. " **πνεῦμα**» («pnyoo'-mah"), accessed June 1, 2023, https://www.blueletterbible.org/lexicon/g4151/kjv/tr/0-1/.

18. *Blue Letter Bible*, s.v. " **εἷς**" ("hice"), accessed June 1, 2023, https://www.blueletterbible.org/lexicon/g1520/kjv/tr/0-1/.

CONTACT INFORMATION

Andrew Wommack Ministries, Inc.
PO Box 3333
Colorado Springs, CO 80934-3333
info@awmi.net
awmi.net

Helpline: 719-635-1111 (available 24/7)

Charis Bible College
info@charisbiblecollege.org
844-360-9577
CharisBibleCollege.org

For a complete list of our offices, visit **awmi.net/contact-us.**

Connect with us on social media.

CHARIS
HEALING
UNIVERSITY

The *Charis Healing University* box-set curriculum is made up of extensive teaching and guided application from trusted Bible teachers Andrew Wommack, Barry Bennett, Carlie Terradez, Carrie Pickett, Daniel Amstutz, Duane Sheriff, and Greg Mohr.

Charis Healing University contains over 60 hours of teaching spread across **forty-eight online video lessons**, six Q&A panel discussions, and several study resources that have been organized into three different sections:

- ***Expect*** will build your faith to believe for healing.
- ***Experience*** will help you know success and receive your healing.
- ***Empower*** will equip you to minister healing to others with confidence.

The *Charis Healing University* box-set curriculum includes **workbooks** for each section, a **USB** containing audio lessons, and access to our **online course**. The online course gives you access to video lessons and printable PDFs for group study.

Go to **awmi.net/HealingU** or call **719-635-1111**.

Item Code: 6012-U

Biblical Worldview

In today's upside-down world, the only solid ground is the Word of God.

 Online Course

 USB

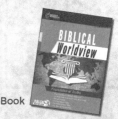 Book

Andrew Wommack's **Biblical Worldview: Foundational Truths** will anchor you on the solid rock of the Bible.

This multimedia curriculum includes 12 online video lessons, a lesson book, and USB audio recordings. It's perfect for home or on-the-go learning!

This course will help you:

- navigate today's world with clarity and conviction
- speak God's truths with compassion and confidence
- impact the lives of those around you
- strengthen your foundation on truth

Visit **awmi.net/BWTruth** or call our Helpline at **719-635-1111** to order *Biblical Worldview: Foundational Truths* today.

Explore our full library of *Biblical Worldview* materials that will help you stand firm on truth.

Go to
awmi.net/BWSeries
to learn more!

CHARIS
BIBLE COLLEGE

God has **more** for you.

Are you longing to find your God-given purpose? At Charis Bible College you will establish a firm foundation in the Word of God and receive hands-on ministry experience to **find, follow,** and **fulfill** your purpose.

Scan the QR code for a free Charis teaching!

CharisBibleCollege.org
Admissions@awmcharis.com
(844) 360-9577

Change your life. **Change the world.**

Don't miss
The Gospel Truth
with Andrew Wommack!

Discover God's unconditional love and grace and see God in a whole new way!

- ▶ Hear the Word of God taught with simplicity and clarity.
- ▶ Understand the true Gospel message and be set free from all kinds of bondages.
- ▶ Learn how to receive your breakthrough.

Go to **awmi.net/video** for local broadcast times or to watch online.